Goal Setting, Motivation, Discipline and Persistence

(Short Guides for Busy Writers)

Brian Jackson

brian@iib.pub
https://iib.pub/brian

Goal Setting, Motivation, Discipline and Persistence   Brian Jackson

Published by IIB Publishing

<u>Sign Up for My Newsletter</u>

Subscribe to my <u>Author Brian Jackson Newsletter</u>!

<u>https://authorbrianjacksonnewsletter.com</u>

Receive **free** training updates via email. Track my progress as I attempt to fully document the writing, self-publishing and marketing world.

Unsubscribe anytime.

4

Table of Contents

1 <u>Introduction</u>

This is a book about achieving your dreams.

It begins by sharing tips and techniques for defining your goals. It then shows you how to start moving by building motivation. Once moving, you must set direction toward your goals and manage your progress using discipline. Persistence will help you overcome challenging obstacles while having a workaround will get you past the insurmountable obstacles. Finally, you start over again at the beginning.

Let's begin achieving your goals by moving forward to the first chapter.

8

2 <u>Goal Setting</u>

In this chapter, we'll examine goal setting, explicitly setting achievable, incremental, and measurable (AIM) goals.

If you're not quite sure what your goals are, pursue your passions. Do you know what I mean?

Consider turning your hobbies into your job. After all, aren't your hobbies what you naturally gravitate to? Aren't those the things that you love? Shouldn't that be the thing that you're doing to make money?

So, what's passion? Maybe you still don't quite understand.

Passion will keep you working and engaged until 2 a.m. because that's what it often takes to achieve great things.

And then there's money.

Money is the ultimate affirmation. Kind words from friends and family are lovely. Reviews and thumbs up are positively fantastic. But having someone lay down their hard-earned cash for something you created is the ultimate validation. Plus, you can spend the money on stuff. That's a dream come true.

If you become good enough at what you're making money at, you can quit your job and do what you love. Isn't that everybody's goal? So, your art versus money. It's an intriguing balancing act.

Next, let's look at what makes a goal achievable.

Achievable goals are realistic. An unachievable goal makes no sense and is often too grand, while achievable goals can be accomplished relatively quickly.

Now, what makes a goal incremental?

The following goal is too grand: I want to be a concert violinist. I want to learn to play the violin, especially if you have yet to begin.

Goals can and should be split into smaller, achievable, incremental, and measurable goals, keeping the ultimate goal in mind.

So, obtaining a violin, learning to play the violin, and joining the community orchestra would all be reasonable incremental or short-term goals for achieving your ultimate goal: becoming a concert violinist.

So, what makes a goal measurable?

A goal is measurable when you can quickly tell whether you have achieved it. The following goal is not measurable. I want to become a star someday. The following is a reinterpretation of that goal to make it measurable. I want to win an Oscar before I'm 30. Notice that this includes the goal of winning an Oscar and the time constraint when I'm 30. This is a reasonably specific goal. And I could tell you whether you achieved it or not.

How about I want to become a bestseller someday versus becoming an Amazon Kindle Top One hundred seller within three years? So, someday has been replaced with three years, and the bestseller has been replaced with the specific Amazon Kindle Top 100 bestseller.

One thing that may help you is creating a hierarchy of goals. Building a hierarchy of goals is one way to keep your goal in sight, as if you'd never forget it, while focusing on your short-term and, thus, more measurable goals.

For instance, I want to become a concert pianist in 10 years. That's my long-term goal. Obtaining a violin this week is a short-term goal. Learning to play violin in a year is another short-term goal. Joining the local orchestra in one year is a short-term goal.

And if it helps, you might want to break your short-term goals into even shorter goals and write them down. Record this stuff. Somehow, writing it down magically makes it real.

My last piece of advice is to remember this when overwhelmed. You can only do one thing at a time. So, remember this. Remember this. Remember this. So, what's your most important goal?

In the next chapter, we'll look at motivation or building momentum.

3 <u>Motivation: Building Momentum</u>

Welcome to my chapter on motivation and building momentum. This chapter will discuss the drive that will help you accomplish your goals. Let's begin by discussing the engine that makes everything possible.

When you're motivated, everything you do seems straightforward. It's as if you have a fire in your belly burning to succeed. Your enthusiasm and your interest in your tasks make time fly. You accomplish more while loving what you do.

I imagine that at some time, you felt motivated in your work and noticed how it improved the entire process. Life is a drag without motivation, and every job is a burden. So, we need motivation to get things done.

The problem comes when we wait for motivation to arrive. The problem with waiting for motivation to arrive is it never will.

Where does motivation come from?

Motivation comes from doing things. Unfortunately, it's easier to do things when we're motivated. This is a classic dilemma or catch-22:

13

We need to be motivated to do things, but we also need to do things to get motivated.

So, what can we do to find the motivation to succeed?

Finding motivation is simple. Do anything, even if it's the wrong thing.

It's hard to get a stalled car moving from a dead stop, while it's much easier to keep it moving once it's rolling. So, the key to motivation is step one. Get yourself moving from a dead stop. Once you're driving, steer yourself.

It doesn't matter if you're going the wrong way. It doesn't matter if you're doing the wrong thing. You're doing something. You have the engine running. You have everything engaged. You're making progress. All you need to do is steer, and that's easy.

So, keep reading this book, but get up and do something once finished. Anything.

Now, how do you stoke the fires of your motivation?

Nothing builds motivation like success.

I want to discuss Swiss cheesing significant goals, problems, or tasks with you. When a goal seems too large to achieve, it's overwhelming and daunting—Swiss cheese is divided into tiny accomplishable steps.

Swiss cheese has holes, so the idea is to take a big chunk of cheese and keep biting holes out of it until the cheese is gone. Take baby steps— another way to look at it. Make corrections as you proceed. It's much easier to change your direction when you're just taking baby steps and going slow. Then, once you figure out where you're going, full bore ahead.

Break your single insurmountable goal into thousands of tiny successes. Allow your baby steps to lead to more experience leaps and bounds.

Now, I want to discuss the importance of to-do lists. I pretty much run my life through to-do lists. Please keep it simple by maintaining your list on paper or in a text file with a text editor. That's what I do. I do everything on the computer, so I have a text file. I have to-do lists on several projects after several goals I'm trying to work on.

Get your tasks out of your mind and onto paper or a file so that you can use your mind for more productive things rather than meditating and trying to remember everything you must do. Please write it down, get it out of your mind, and use your mind for other things.

Order your list in dependency order. For instance, if I want to wash the car well, I better hose it down first, apply the suds, dry it, rinse it, and dry it again. So, make your list in order of dependency of tasks, but within that order, it is by priority, so you're working on the most important things.

Checking things off your list can be extremely rewarding. This is one of the things I love about lists. Sometimes, I put straightforward tasks on my to-do list to check them off.

Review and update your to-do list routinely to ensure where you're going and work on the most critical tasks to get you there.

Meanwhile, keep your goals in mind. This is so important, and I'm reminding you about what problem you're trying to solve so I can tell you this story.

I worked for a long time at Cisco Systems, and it seemed like the longer I worked there, the more my job became going into meetings and stating what problem I was trying to solve. Everybody had lists of tasks and things we should do, but nobody could remember what we were trying to accomplish. Don't fall into that mistake. Keep your goals in mind while maintaining your to-do list.

Now, I want to discuss the secret to blocking distractions with you, and here it is: Draw the line and defend it.

Stephen Covey divided tasks into those that are not very high priority but are extremely important in your life and those that are high priority. So, you're constantly hit all day long with "I got to do this," "I got to do this," and "I got to do this," and you're never hit with achieving those primary goals because those aren't as important, but they are essential in your life.

Your goals are the most important things. That's what you should be working on.

So, allocate a portion of your life to mundane tasks, such as going to work, making dinner, taking care of the kids, or whatever constitutes a high-priority task. You have to do tasks daily but also dedicate time to your goals—those low-priority, high-essential functions in your life.

Now, I want to talk with you about the empowerment of doing something, anything.

Motivation comes from success. If you start doing things and accomplishing them, you will be motivated. Then, you can direct that motivation to your goals, even if you're getting it from doing things that have nothing to do with them.

If you suffer from depression and you're lying in bed, pat yourself on the back if you get out of bed, shower, and brush your teeth in the morning. It's a minor accomplishment, but it will build motivation and get you to your goals.

And, of course, check it off the list. Bang! There we go. I love that. So, if you have something you're working on and complete it, check it off your list. You won't believe how good that's going to make you feel.

Now, we are building momentum. As you do things and experience success, you'll begin to build momentum until you become unstoppable.

Along the way, things will remind you how vulnerable you are and that you are indeed stoppable. And that's where discipline and persistence come into play to get you through the tough times. And we're about to talk about discipline in the next chapter.

4 <u>Discipline: Directed Momentum</u>

This is my chapter on discipline or directed momentum. In the previous chapter, we looked at building momentum. Now, we're going to look at directing it towards our goals.

Directed momentum is the concept of having momentum and guiding it toward specific objectives. It's about being intentional and focused in your actions.

You've established your goals and built momentum. Now it's time to put your head down in thoughtless pursuit of progress. Or is it? What about steering?

Discipline involves periodically checking to ensure you're moving in the right direction while maintaining momentum. Another word for discipline is management.

Yes, it's time to get to work, but in an orderly fashion.

Now, I want to discuss the importance of rewards or why we do what we do. You will fail if you keep beating yourself to succeed and never acknowledge your accomplishments. We do everything we can to gain rewards. Virtually everything we do is selfish in a way.

Mother Teresa worked hard toward the selfish reward of helping others. If she hadn't done it, she wouldn't have been able to sleep at night. She did it because she had no choice.

Reward yourself for every accomplishment. That's what good managers do.

Remember to review and update your goals and supporting to-do list regularly. I'm just putting this in there as a reminder.

We've already talked about it several times. Part of management is reviewing your to-do list regularly.

Now, let's talk about adding stretch goals. What's a stretch goal?

We all have our goals. But don't we also have those unstated secret goals that would thrill us to no end if we achieved them? Those are your stretch goals.

So set your goals, but consider what would be just one step beyond. Often, our most impressive accomplishments are achieved via our stretch goals.

For instance, you might set a goal to walk 10,000 steps today. But what if you pushed yourself to aim for 12,000 steps? That's a good stretch goal.

Or, if you're a content creator, you might set a goal to record 30 minutes of video today. But what if you challenged yourself to aim for 45 minutes? That would be excellent.

Or, even more practical, I will write 1,000 words today. But 2,000 words would be more in the direction I'd like to go. Stretch goals often challenge us to go beyond the routine and take our accomplishments to the next level.

I want to discuss monitoring, maintaining, and improving your performance with you. Another aspect of management involves monitoring and maintaining your ability to perform. So, by all means, get to your meeting on time and stop to smell the roses occasionally.

And how do you monitor your performance?

That's simple. Health and mood.

You are not headed toward achieving your goals if you are unhealthy and unhappy. Your performance is terrible. You score an F.

If, on the other hand, you're feeling great, your mood is upbeat, and you see a positive future, you're doing great. Keep on going. Your gut should tell you when things are off track. Remember, you're pursuing your passions with passion. Nothing should be wrong unless something is wrong. So, monitor and adjust as needed.

Part of management is monitoring and changing things to optimize your health and mood or, to summarize, all things balance.

Passion is about balancing your life and directing your momentum toward your goals. And that's the end of this chapter.

In the next chapter, I'll discuss persistence or overcoming obstacles.

5 <u>Persistence: Sustained Momentum</u>

In this chapter, I want to discuss persistence or sustained momentum. Now that you've built up your momentum and directed it, the last thing you want is something to stand in your way.

So, what is persistence?

Persistence involves overcoming the most common daily interruptions and the significant life challenges between you and your goals.

Before I begin, I want to make a slight aside about the unfair advantage of stubbornness.

My wife is stubborn. I call it an unfair advantage. Then again, I suppose I'm stubborn in my way. Aren't we all stubborn? There's a lot to be said for stubbornness. Proceed to face adversity, but that will only get you so far.

To avoid daily interruptions, you need to carve out your own time and enforce a schedule to make time for you to achieve your most important goals. It would be best if you did this. This is probably the most critical point in the whole book.

Make your own time a daily routine. Then, go so far as to announce your daily routine to your friends, family, and others and insist they respect it. I do not doubt that when you explain your daily routine's goals and importance, they will respect it.

Here are the first Golden Brian Jackson quotes from this class. Check this out: "Life is nothing but time, so why not defend your time as if you're defending your life?"

Think about it. Are you living if you're not using your time to achieve your passions and goals? Maybe you're just existing.

So, unless there's blood, accept no interruptions to your daily routine of making time to achieve your goals.

Another vital technique I want to discuss is keeping and envisioning that goal.

To maintain your focus, I recommend that you use a technique used by athletes the world over, and that is to envision yourself achieving your goals. There's something magical that happens. Who knows how the brain works? Some connection gets made by seeing yourself achieve your goals.

Now, the next thing I want to talk to you about is that overcoming obstacles is essential, but I want you to speak about reality instead of smacking or hyping yourself. Don't put yourself down, but don't delude yourself. So, persistence is excellent, but when your path is blocked, it's blocked. Don't fool yourself.

And how do you get around that blocked path?

Have multiple irons in the fire.

So, how do you overcome the insurmountable obstacle?

You step around it. If it's insurmountable, don't keep beating your head against it.

Talk reality to yourself at some point, and develop multiple alternate paths toward your goal. Swiftly discard the losers and continue your pursuit of the winners.

Here's another, the second great quote from at least this chapter: "The only consequence of failure is eventual success."

Think about it. Keep on going. This kind of thinking makes persistence work and drives you forward, but also remember that there are impossible goals, so step around them. Once the obstacle is cleared, you know what I want you to do?

You're right. Lower your head again and proceed toward your goal. Be dogged, be persistent, and achieve your goals. I'll see you in the next chapter.

6 <u>Rinse and Repeat</u>

In this final chapter of the process, we'll cover the rinse-and-repeat step. To execute this, you return to goal setting and start over again. I put together this simple presentation for those who still need help.

- Repeat.
- And...repeat.
- Stop when you accomplish your goal, or you are dead.
- If you are not dead, set a new goal.
- And...repeat.
- And keep going until you are dead.

I know it's crude, but I hope it clarifies my point.

7 <u>Conclusion</u>

Set achievable, incremental and measurable goals based on your passions. Try to balance your passions with making money so that you can someday make a living pursuing them.

Write down your goals.

Do anything to gain momentum, then steer your actions toward your goals. Let nothing get in your way as you dodge insurmountable obstacles.

When you achieve a goal, start again with a new one.

Sign Up for My Newsletter

Subscribe to my Author Brian Jackson Newsletter!

https://authorbrianjacksonnewsletter.com

Receive **free** training updates via email. Track my progress as I attempt to fully document the writing, self-publishing and marketing world.

Unsubscribe anytime.